Birds, Bees, and Me

Birds, Bees, and Me

Songs of Praise and Lament by a Gay Christian

Delivered April 16th 2022.
Abidemi Shitta-Bey · (48)· MBHs.
Oritsemenyi Esimaje (45) KC.

COLLIN BRICE

Foreword by Trey Celaya

GOD is LOVE. 1st John 4:16.

"He Was always patient and Kind even When I did nothing but seemingly Waste his time."

"Entirely God's Kindness."
(Page. 16.)

RESOURCE *Publications* · Eugene, Oregon

Resource Publications
An Imprint of Wipf and Stock Publishers
199 W. 8th Ave., Suite 3
Eugene, OR 97401

www.wipfandstock.com

PAPERBACK ISBN: 978-1-7252-6378-9
HARDCOVER ISBN: 978-1-7252-6371-0
EBOOK ISBN: 978-1-7252-6372-7

Manufactured in the U.S.A.   04/16/20

CONTENTS

FOREWORD

WHEN I MET COLLIN, I noticed pretty quickly that he was different, but perhaps in a way that only a few pick up on. His mannerisms, his inflection, the way his walk looked more like a glide as he floated through a room, his torso perfectly straight. His curly, unkempt hair gave the impression that he never knew quite how to make it look presentable, and he was just trying his best.

Nonetheless, he knew how to blend in well despite his oddities, and he was possibly the most hospitable and gifted host I've ever witnessed, always gracefully manipulating people into being his friend. It starts by meeting them, then he reaches out on social media, gets their number, and invites them to either a tennis match, an intimate gathering at his home, or a one-on-one dinner if he gets the impression that they're a decently warm person. I think he particularly likes the challenge of getting shy types to open up to him. That's what he did with me, anyway.

I met him at a friend's house, and before I knew it, he was inviting me to come play video games and getting me to open up about my darkest secrets and deepest insecurities. I was willing to do that though, because I felt safe with him. I suppose he sensed that he could feel safe with me as well, because he told me his secrets not long after. Being entrusted with those secrets came with the responsibility of playing a particular role in his life, a level of dependability. I signed myself up to be his Advocate. To be present when no one else would, when he didn't know how to be there for himself. To be someone that saw him as he sincerely was. To be someone that knew.

I can remember the feeling of answering a call from him on several occasions, always at night, always at the same hiking trail. Before I could say hello, or sometimes, "What's up Big Stinky Daddy?" (a term of endearment) I could hear crying on the other end. It usually took him at least 20 seconds to even say my name. The sobs could almost be mistaken for uncontrollable laughter — the same vulnerability as always, the same shamelessness. But the grief was palpable and uncomfortable.

On my end, there was always a striking tension of helplessness and obligation. I was often frustrated that I didn't feel I had the mental or emotional capacity to be present for him. Getting a call like this meant I had to drop whatever I was doing and drive almost 30 minutes to the hiking trail, and sit in his car. He sobbed uncontrollably for a while, making my shirt well acquainted with his snot and tears. Before we parted ways, I'd make sure he was calm enough to go home and sleep—probably due to exhaustion more than having found a sense of peace. And then I would drive home, feeling exhausted myself.

After a few nights like these, I learned to simply say, "I'm on my way" as soon as I could tell he needed me. Sometimes I knew before I even answered the phone.

But I would always go. When I pulled up to the dark trail, under the whisper of the trees, his car was usually the only one in the parking lot. He drives a Prius, making the stereotype of "gay guy driving a Prius" one of the only gay stereotypes he actually fits (besides really enjoying musicals). Occasionally, there would be another car in the parking lot opposite from us.

He told me once that kids would go there often to fornicate in their cars. How odd that a couple would sneak over to the same trail to have raunchy sex, and across the parking lot, someone was there alongside them, crying alone because he would never know that same intimacy with another person. I'm sure there's a metaphor there, somewhere.

As I approached, I could hear his muffled crying becoming louder. Intimidated, I would take a breath and say a quick, silent prayer, trying to muster the courage to step in. It felt so unnatural to act as someone's support. I often thought: "I'm ill-equipped for this, to say the least. Is there such a thing as empathy training? Are there any courses I can sign up for?" I would open his car door and sit in the passenger seat. He would desperately slump over the console and hold me tightly like he had been lost in an abyss for days, and I was the first real thing he could cling to. The only piece of driftwood in an open sea. The only light at the end of a very grim and ordinary weekday.

When I pick up a book, I'm looking for a stretch of the imagination. I'm looking to escape and get lost in exuberant stories and landscapes that I would frankly rather live in than my own world. I want fantasy and everything magical that comes with it. Yet, the words in this book, however poignant or seemingly exaggerated, are not at all far from the truth. His world is just as hopeful and desperate and beautiful and sad as is stated. You may very well know that to be true from your own experience.

To immerse yourself in these pages is to immerse yourself in the world of another. It is to grab the hand of someone who will lead you through a painfully honest experience. But I expect that as you take this leap of faith, as you risk your worldview becoming a little broader than you previously thought possible, you'll dive headfirst into the stories of a stranger, and by the time you come up for air, he will feel like a familiar friend.

Maybe you'll see that friend in someone you knew before. Someone you grew up with or went to school with. Someone you never got to know and always overlooked. There is still time to know them. It's not too late to befriend someone you weren't sure that you could love.

The reward is this: when you risk love, you gain the opportunity to be loved in return. And it is always worth it. The late-night calls to console them at the hiking trail, the weight of being one of the only people that they've let into the deepest darkest parts of their soul, whatever it may look like, I wouldn't trade for anything. It is in being a friend that I have become a friend. In fact, I've found that is the only way in which to love and to be loved.

Loving Collin has challenged my identity and my pride as a heterosexual male. Will friends think differently of me if they see him cuddled on me like a puppy as we lounge on the couch? Will strangers give me strange looks when they see that I'm walking with someone dressed in clothes deemed less masculine than mine? Can I greet him with a kiss without feeling like I need to say "no homo" afterward? Maybe, maybe not, but does it really matter when we're talking about a human being? Should we discard the humanity of another to keep our image and reputation intact? I believe that implicitly answering that question with a "yes" has led to disproportionately high suicide rates in the LGBTQ+ population, and there's got to be a better way. There has to be a way we can love the "other" that doesn't end in condemnation or religious platitudes or overdoses or some other horrific thing. I don't know what the answer is, but I suspect that it will look a little different in every case.

And as this stranger becomes your friend, you will become a better friend as well. In becoming that friend, you practice empathy. My request to you, reader, is this: As you read these stories, take perhaps your first step in the path of compassion. Become a friend to a stranger. They need you. And you need them more than you know.

Trey Celaya
Drummer for Invent Animate,
The Advocate

PREFACE

HI THERE! MY NAME is Collin Brice. As a former pastor's kid in a Southern church, and as someone still trying to sort out what the Bible is, what my spirituality is, and what my sexuality is, I've wrestled with lots of diverse questions. Many of these will come up in this book, but to my Christian and theology lovers who are reading, I want to stress that I am not trying to write a theologically rich book here.

This book is my story, and it mirrors the stories of others who dare not share at the risk of their experiences being deconstructed or invalidated by the systematic and cerebral schemas . . . schemas which so often tell me that I believe lies or that I don't understand God or the Gospel in the right way.

My story responds to you in the same way I personally do: Even if that is the case, even if I don't understand, I really don't care. In the loneliness and grey parts of my sexuality, your systems and binaries often don't work for me. I've had to find my own jagged route, which is full of experiences most people who preach to me will never understand except through the eyes of someone else.

I ask that you graciously exercise that with me—feel and see things through my eyes as best you can. Weigh the logic and truth if you must, but understand that my frequent sobs of loneliness and confusion cannot do the same. Those moments are unable to consider that one day I might be whole and complete, that one day this won't matter. Those moments bring only unbearable isolation within a community of mostly Christians who don't understand that my faith costs me much more than I let on.

There is truth to be found, even in a mess. I hope my mess lends to you—in a raw, real way—the answers to some of your questions. However, my experience tells me that a deeper understanding of a thing tends to lead us to ten times more questions. I expect that to be the case here.

Another goal I want to emphasize here is that I don't intend to deal with the morality of homosexuality. There are plenty of good books and resources for that, and I find myself unsure of what I think about it. All I assert in this book is that, up to this point, I have decided it is for my benefit to live a celibate lifestyle. Some will criticize everything about that stance, but hasty, dogmatic stances from others regarding my sexuality is something that has wounded me. I am not here to speak for anyone else.

At the end of most chapters, you will find a story about a girl named Ana. Ana is a true story based on a few friends who were, like me, forced into sexual shame by circumstances out of their control. I hope it gives you something additional to reflect on as you hear my story.

I have gay friends who are celibate, gay friends who have partners, and gay friends who are in heterosexual marriages. This is a niche topic, but I'm taking lengths to make it as accessible to Southern Baptist Christians as it is to my LGBTQ+ loved ones. Everyone must decide who and what they love most. I hope truth plays a part in my own decisions, but as I've found out, truth is a tricky thing.

ACKNOWLEDGMENTS

I WANT TO THANK Mrs. Edna Earney, who had no idea what she was getting herself into when she first agreed to copy edit this project of mine. Your encouragement and desire to improve my writing voice the past decade is one of the reasons I felt confident enough to begin recording this journey in the first place.

Special thanks to every friend who had listened and loved me fiercely, even when their upbringing, surroundings, or church explicitly told them not to. Trey, Cal, Emily, David, Josh H., Josh D., Rachel, Bethany, Rhett, Trent, Sam, Amy, Windsor, Mason, Abby, and many others, your embraces are the fire that compels me to publish this memoir in the first place and are daily reminders that God really is good.

And finally, thank you to James and Matt, who are mentors of mine. After going through so much unsafety, you two have been safe places when I was ready to give up on the church altogether. The sanctuaries you two provided for me have nurtured so many of my wounds found on these pages.

CHAPTER 1

A MEMORY CAME BACK to me this week. It's one I've had to verify with a few friends to make sure it was real, but the fog cleared as I've allowed myself closer to the recount. When it came to me, I thought, I'm not sure this happened. It seemed too overtly evil.

No.

Evil is too strong a word, I think, or not strong enough. It seemed too nothing: without love or any consideration for the vulnerable at all.

Pastor Alan Stockman was the youth pastor of the youth group I attended for most of middle school and all of high school. He was confident, collected, charismatic, and a fantastic singer. Going to a charismatic church meant that "prophetic" voices were highly regarded and practiced regularly. It is essentially thought of to be the act of God speaking through someone to share wisdom, usually with an individual or a group of people.

"I have a word for someone," Pastor Alan would say as he scanned over the audience. Every student would be still, half hoping that Alan's eyes would stop on them and half hoping they would not. With a mystic air in his voice, he would give his "word" to someone in the audience. He'd describe in scary detail something that the audience member had only confided in a few people. Then Alan would offer some encouragement or wisdom to them.

Ten years later, I'm not sure what to make of it, and many of my peers feel the same way. We can all acknowledge the arrogance and manipulation that was horrendously present during many of those services . . . but Alan was also utterly correct. He knew things that he shouldn't know. He'd prophesy (or whatever you'd like to call it) in detail to both strangers and regulars with jarring accuracy.

Ultimately, Alan loved to possess secret knowledge. It made him valuable to us; it made us hang on to his every word. He kicked off the prophetic time with the phrase, "God is telling me that there is someone in this room who . . ."

"There is someone in the room who got accepted into college tonight. Can you raise your hand?"

One senior in the back raised his hand.

Alan looked at him and smiled. "I'm sensing that God is setting you up for a lot of financial responsibility. That is exciting but could end up being the death of you. You need to start preparing for that now. Make budgets and figure out how you're going to honor God with your money," Alan would say with urgency.

That is one of many memories I have of those hyper-spiritual services, but not the memory that came to my mind so vividly a few days ago.

I was seventeen at the time, a senior in high school. Despite having acknowledged that I was gay by this point in life, I had only told two mentors of mine, one of which encouraged me to talk to my youth pastor about it. Even at that time, my intuition told me this advice might be questionable; it was sensitive and vulnerable information for me to share. Still, another part of me thought, if anyone can help me be straight, it will be Alan. I already saw him as having pseudo-mystic powers. I'd seen people be healed, prophesied over, speak in tongues . . . why not see if this is what could "cure" me?

So I told him. Our conversation escapes my memory, but I do remember him telling me that he believed I could be healed, that I could be straight. I nodded my head to him in wordless agreement.

The next Wednesday, as anticipated, another wave of mystic air blew into the room. Some would call it the Holy Spirit. The sermon was about healing (as charismatic church sermons often are!), and Pastor Alan was on a roll. He was just then at the climax of his sermon, speaking of how God can change our lives when he paused.

"God is telling me there is someone in this room who struggles with homosexuality, and I just want to encourage that person to keep . . . "

My heart stopped; I turned to stone. I avoided eye contact with Alan. I didn't want him to interpret anything as an encouragement to get more explicit. I don't remember what advice he offered to me as if it matters.

The only thing that mattered was protecting my identity. I had told some friends that Alan and I were meeting the previous week. Would they put two and two together? My only chance tonight was to delete myself completely, to take out all emotions and facial expressions that could indicate the "prophetic word" was about me. Thank God Pastor Alan didn't use my name. He left it anonymous.

I remember talking to Sidney, one of the more popular girls, after the church service ended.

"I wonder who Alan was talking about when he said someone was homosexual," she had wondered out loud to me, "I think it's probably about Maya from the softball team. She's always given me a lesbian vibe."

She had given an "ugh!" of disgust after finishing her thought.

I laughed, agreed, and dissociated entirely for the night.

I walked out of church, relatively unchanged. Alan was still my pastor who knew best, and I put my faith in his words: that I could be healed and straight. Years later, however, I realized for the first time a few days ago that he did both of our souls a disservice.

He used my confidence to feign secret knowledge and appear prophetic in a manner that not only betrayed my trust but abused the sinister power dynamic at play.

He knew I could not say anything, or even appear upset unless I wanted to risk outing myself as gay. He knew how harshly and passionately the topic of homosexuality fell on southern, teenage, Christian ears. He was able to once again steal his audience for the evening in a way that would have everyone talking for weeks. Well, everyone except me.

Alan was a catalyst for me, clarifying who I was: an outlier secretly living on the margins while pretending I was not. I was a preacher's plaything, helping him appear holy, diverse, and discerning as he left me to go back into hiding. I was somebody, but not somebody we should be talking about unless we found the proper time and place, for I with no mask was "improper." From the margins, I could interact with everyone as long as we pretended the margins did not exist.

It often feels like I am in isolation, but can pretend that I'm not . . . like everyone lives on a magnificent trail where they can camp and shop and have sex. But I must withdraw each night to a clearing in the woods, an unattended acre that is paradoxically both lifeless and overgrown.

I chose to stick tightly to my disguise, refusing to consider how my sexuality would alienate me. I don't think Alan and I spoke about it ever again. I ran to my Acre.

THE ACRE

Hello there!

I have met you in these woods before. Actually, I have watched you many times along this worn Trail where the beauty found in common ground is easy to delight in. The road is lit up with candles and lamps, and the dancing at night brings people to life. Its stories of good and evil unite listeners, evoking both tears and laughter. Lovers meet for the first time in these woods, and they never leave.

And why would they leave this wonderful place? The joy found on the Trail is as tangible as grass, trees, or any other solid thing! I've seen it. Neighbors become mothers and fathers, uncles and aunts. The trees and animals yield enough work and food for everyone.

The running water always roars but never threatens. It washes the days off of workers just as well as it washes the nights off of lovers. It glistens in the sun as fish leap, beckoning fishermen to come spend their days here, poles in hand, hats over face . . .

With so many hands to help the community thrive, there is never a weed too evasive for someone to catch, never a ripe fruit neglected until it rots. Everything is tended to, and everything is used.

And, oh, the stories you will hear along The Trail! Children and elderly alike warm up by fires as they animate a spectrum of topics too vast to describe: outcasts who overcome every obstacle, characters who forgive beyond what is forgivable, women who lead a country, men who put the weight of the world on their shoulders . . . there is something for everyone who lives on The Trail, and each resident can find something to resonate with. There's no lack of understanding.

Lack is rarely a word used to describe this part of the woods at all, but when it is, when one finds himself in need, everyone makes movements to help. When one finds that there isn't enough food, neighbors cook a feast for anyone who can come. Where illness and tragedy steal a life, comfort takes every shape imaginable as The Trail grieves with those who are grieving.

The Trail is an attentive hospital, a good religion, a loving counselor, a beloved identity.

It's your home. Your tent is set up close by, close to those who love you, to those who understand you. And aren't those synonymous? Or at least co-dependent? Is one ever loved without being understood? Can a person ever understand someone's heart, truly empathize with them, and not love them? It is known; empathy is oxygen on the trail. A poor quality of either leads to sickness. An absence of either brings death.

I've heard how peacefully you sleep at night. There is no danger to prepare for. There is no worry about tomorrow, although excitement and camaraderie beckon the sun to come up sooner than it would. And if there is a worry, the resources at hand always prove more than enough.

How I wish I could bring my own tent to The Trail! I have tried a couple of times, but there is no room for me without pushing someone else out, and wouldn't that choke the spirit of The Trail? To be present is to resist someone else. I have worked it out over and over in my head, but every outcome would lead us to a flaccidity where there was once life, a stagnancy where there was once movement. It won't work. For me to thrive there, your own must suffer the discomfort of great change.

No, I live at The Acre a few miles that way. It's hard to find unless you know where to go, and, I'll be honest, it's nothing like The Trail.

I have seen people there, sure, but they are not glowing from candlelight nor dancing like they are here. We tend to look a little malnourished, and very grey. The dark circles under our eyes speak loudly of the restless nights endured from hunger pangs and defending against angry mosquitoes and gnats. But we make do. Most are nomads, moving along on their own journey after a time.

We don't really make eye contact with each other there, much less speak as family or friends. Understanding someone takes too much time and energy when you're just trying to survive. In fact, the last guy I gave a good look at only hung around for a few days before he ate what was left of my food and headed out. He was an asshole.

There's no running water at The Acre, per se, but I'll occasionally find a still pond to bathe in (I don't think I smell that bad), and usually someone from your neck of the woods is kind enough to give me some drinking water. I do give those fried fish a lot of thought—the ones I've seen your neighbors cook. But really, I don't have many needs that aren't met! I'm grateful.

In fact, I borrowed some books from you guys a couple weeks ago so that I could figure out how to grow these damn fruit trees. I did everything the books said to do, but my trees still aren't doing so hot. There's nothing in your books about problems growing these. I guess you've never had any issues growing them? I wonder if it has to do with the running water in your orchard . . . It doesn't matter; I already gave up. I can only do so much when there's one of me.

Sure, The Acre is a lifeless mess, but it just needs some tender love and care. Given quality time and experimenting, I think we might even be better than The Trail! How does *that* sound?

I'm hoping some of these nomads will come back and help me. Lord knows I don't have the best problem solving skills when it comes to . . . wait a second! How about you come with me? That would be double the brains, double the help, double the family (so far, it's just me).

Won't you come with me? There isn't a path to get to The Acre, so I'll have to take you. Well, there is a path, but it isn't paved, and only I have walked it, so it's still kinda hard to see.

Won't you come with me? Your books and knowledge of The Trail won't apply much to my little Acre, but maybe you can help me anyway! Trial and error, baby. I know that's a scary thought, but I've already completed a lot of trials (mostly errors) and I can share with you what I've learned. I've survived this long, haven't I?

Won't you come with me? I see your shoes weren't made for the thorny terrain, but neither were mine. These wounds on my legs have already shown me where many of the most unruly areas are, so you won't have to feel them yourself. There's no hospital, but we'll take care of each other. Just take my hand.

No one has mapped out the area around The Acre yet, but won't you just come with me? Take yourself off of your own trail. Let your mind take some strides away from the customary steps you've known, and consider with me that there might be more out here. Please, let me show you.

Let preconceived ideas, which raised you from birth and fostered your every step, be set down for a second. Tread through these vines and the tall grass. I promise they don't mean danger, just unfamiliarity. I know those seemed pretty similar to me at first too . . . actually, I have a confession.

I've never actually taken anyone out here. Sure, some of your people have peered into The Acre, and have made guesses about what is growing (or what isn't). But they're usually wrong. And lately something new has shown up. A voice has been crying out to me at night. I sit up in my dirt-floored tent to listen.

"Who are you?" I asked the voice.

It didn't answer back, not in words anyway. His tone gives away his identity. I was told a long time ago that he'd be here, demanding to be told a story. His silhouette is crafted by my long nights crying alone, by my failures to make anything here grow, and by my aching to live with you on The Trail. It forms a misshapen monster demanding to be revered.

He wants a sacrifice. He wants my heart, my voice.

He's my silence, everything I haven't shared with you or the nomads or even really thought about myself. I spent many years praying he wouldn't come, and these last few nights have been the longest of my life.

But can I tell you a secret?

With you here, I'm not afraid of him anymore. I want him to leave so that I can sleep, and maybe make something in that damn Acre grow. I want to tell him a story, and satisfy his appetite for good. I know this doesn't make sense to you right now.

Won't you come with me?

FIFTH GRADE

"We're not going to church today" Christy Cox told her daughter, avoiding eye contact.

Ana gave her a puzzled look. Growing up a daughter of a head pastor, she knew that her presence was more than a leisure; it was a duty. In fact, Ana's absence often stirred up talk amongst the members.

"Is Ana sick today?" they would ask.

"I sure hope she isn't struggling in math like her sister always did. Is she home studying?"

She wasn't bothered by any of the talk. Ten-year-old naiveté shone blissfully through each week, but she was also just incredibly patient. The pastoral duties thrown onto the youngest daughter gave her joy and purpose. Often her three older siblings would fill her in on the pettiness of their community at Fellowship Bible Church, the church that their father was over, but it never evoked more than a smirk from Ana.

Christy was recently confronted about letting her daughters watch The Oscars the night it aired.

"I don't know, Chris," another mom said. "That show had a lot of really graphic parts."

Ignoring that the only way this particular church member could have known that The Oscars was playing would be to walk by the side of the house and peer through the window, Christy smiled and thanked her for her concern. Ana rolled her eyes, but knew it would blow over in a day. It was all part of the job.

Ana's best friend Dalton may as well have been born in the church building with her. They were inseparable. Both mothers have baby pictures displayed in their homes of the two children lying on a couch together, Ana sleeping and Dalton trying to bite his own foot. Ana prayed for each member of her church every night a blessing that she recited by memory:

"May the Lord bless you and keep you. May he make his face shine down upon you and be gracious unto you. May the Lord turn his countenance towards you, and give you peace. In Jesus name, amen."

It was from the book of Numbers, but the original source could have been her dad as far as Ana was concerned. Her father would pray it over Ana every night as she went to sleep. After he kissed his daughter and turned off the lights, Ana would repeat the same prayer with all of her community in mind. The church who had helped raise her would receive a fifth grader's blessings not muttered begrudgingly, as is the manner of many pastors' kids, but with fierce care and delight.

"Jesus really loves me," Ana would often think to herself simply as she looked around her world. That day, however, she was content with not going to church.

"That's okay. I think I'm getting sick," Ana told her mom.

Her forehead was heating up, and her face was flushing. It didn't seem like the typical allergy attacks begotten by springtime. The next day, her doctor confirmed that it was the flu. Ana was to be bed-ridden and stay home from school until further notice.

Most unfortunate to Ana was that Wednesday was her birthday. She was turning eleven, and wanted to celebrate with her friends at school and at FBC's Wednesday night service. But alas, the fever was slow to dissipate, and she was doomed to celebrate on the couch while enduring another viewing of Rugrats in Paris. There was nothing wrong with the movie, but monotony was wearing on her. She missed human interaction. The birthday girl wasn't just patient and kind, she was friendly and extroverted to a fault.

Isolation was torture. Each hour she endured apart from friends was an hour that drained her of even more fortitude. Ana sluggishly made her way down the stairs onto the living room couch.

"He's fired," she heard her mom say from the kitchen. ". . . I don't know, but we'll keep you updated."

Ana was perceptive enough to know those were alarming words, but Mrs. Cox didn't offer her daughter any clarification or comfort. She continued to pace in the other room and dialed another number.

"They fired him," she said to the second person. "I love you. Thanks for everything."

She hung up. The atmosphere felt urgent. Ana's mind raced quickly, but she didn't know where to make it run to.

"Is dad still a pastor?" she thought.

Ana's dad had a few jobs, as pastors often need to do in order to make ends meet, so it was confusing to even begin assuming something specific. After a few more puzzling calls, Christy came and sat across from her youngest daughter.

"Daddy doesn't know if he wants to be with me anymore. The church fired him from being a pastor. He's gone camping to think about everything and take some time to himself."

Her mother pulled in closer. She was an incredibly nurturing woman, and a mother to all, but her words put a wall between her and her youngest. The air was tense, and had sent Ana stoically into a state of fight or flight.

Both Ana and her mother were silent. A ticking clock in the living room was the only sound until the AC kicked on.

"Oh . . . okay," Ana finally replied.

It wasn't the most appropriate response, but she wasn't sure what would be appropriate for the moment. Pastors' kids hone the skill very quickly to know what to say, and when to say it. They are born into a battle of poised pragmatism, often with lasting consequences. The battle can serve to embitter some and steady others, but this particular minister's daughter needed some time to think. She spent the next hour staring at the TV, not absorbing any of the dialogue or plot. Her mom came back in with the newest Pokemon game in a gift bag. Her older brothers had introduced Pokemon to

Ana before she knew how to read, and she had begged for Pokemon Emerald when was released. But at that particular moment Ana had forgotten it was her birthday. She plugged it into her Gameboy Advance and let it distract her for a bit.

The next week, Ana still hadn't seen her dad, but she was feeling better about everything. The shock had at least worn off. She didn't ask questions, and answers weren't offered by anyone in the family. The walls could have exploded from the pulsing tension that week. She asked her mom if she could still go to church. Ana had been lonely and missed the church that she often referred to as her family. Mrs. Cox looked away for a few seconds.

"Okay," her mom said.

It seemed like there was something else she wanted to say.

Christy Cox pulled to the front of the church building to drop her daughter off.

"I'll be back to pick you up after service is over," she said before letting Ana out of the car. "I love you."

Ana waved goodbye. She wasn't sure why her mom wouldn't still come to church just because her dad wasn't the pastor anymore. It didn't make sense. These were still the same people the Coxes had always known. She ran into Mr. Aaron on the way to Sunday School. Mr. Aaron was Dalton's dad, and had hosted Ana for playdates roughly every other weekend since she was two.

"Ana!" Mr. Aaron said.

It seemed less like a greeting and more like something else.

"What are you doing here?" he added quickly and with slightly more authority and stability in his voice.

"Oh, hi Mr. Aaron! Just going to Sunday School," Ana replied overly pleasantly in an effort to diffuse the tension she sensed.

Mr. Aaron didn't reply, but began walking the opposite direction with a little more speed. By the time Ana had made it to Sunday School, Mr. Aaron and an elder at the church came in and pulled her out of the room. They sat her on the counter in the kitchen beside the sanctuary. To her right was a cabinet filled with all kinds of first aid supplies that had helped heal her from playground injuries over the years. To her left was the communion trays. They contained juice and bread to consume– an age old sacrament that allowed one to consider the freedom and love Jesus had offered on the cross. Ana and her friends would eat the leftovers after service, which felt to them like an even more sacred tradition.

"With your mom and your dad gone, I think it's time you get going," Mr. Aaron said.

He seemed more composed and rehearsed than minutes before when Ana had seen him, no longer shoehorning leadership into his demeanor, but simply confident in his convictions. Both men in the room smiled at Ana as if trying to comfort her, an "I know this is a difficult situation" look, not without sympathy. It felt to the now eleven-year-old girl, too bright for her age, a bitter sort of irony to see their warm, familiar faces as their words seared forever on her heart. They handed her the phone.

When she finally re-entered the car with her mom, a defeated silence entered as well. There was a realization, with sadness this time. As the daughter of her father, she must bear the mistakes, anger, and sins of her family. It was a role not ever taught to her but somehow expected by every adult: every father figure and mother figure who had raised and loved her. She was abandoned. She looked back at her old church one last time as they drove home.

CHAPTER 2

It's as if I have a perpetually broken bone or torn muscle, not one that is too important. I can still attend school, go to work, even jog, but the pain is there. It persists, slows me down, fogs my mind a bit. I have to rest more than my peers, massaging the knots out of the rest of my body, which compensates for the weakness.

Not having a scan or x-ray to diagnose the problem, I thought perhaps this was what growing up looked like. Maybe the growing pains were lingering, or something needed time to heal. All I knew was that walking with a limp gets boring and tiresome. My subconscious assured me this wouldn't last forever.

Some days are worse than others. On my bad ones, I am stoic, blunt, unmoving. On my good days, I hardly notice the pain at all.

Of course, this metaphor breaks down quickly, because a broken bone or torn muscle can be repaired. It's certainly painful, but restorable and full of potential, especially for young people. But my attraction to men is part of my DNA. The neural connections seem to have set up camp for good. They're staying, no matter how hard I'd like them to make some new pathways.

THIRTEEN YEARS OLD

Around the age of thirteen, I wasn't even half convinced that the feelings I had towards other boys in my Christian school were gay feelings. You might not believe me (especially if you're straight, I imagine), but I think it probably took years for me to realize what I was doing and feeling was homosexual. It's an ignorance that I nod to, but don't feel shame for. I think someone failed me along the way, both as a Christian and as a human.

Perhaps my dad thought conversations about my manhood would be too awkward, or that the private school system would take care of it. Perhaps my health teacher decided to skip that chapter because my class was too immature to discuss something that "everyone already knew." Perhaps The Church thought that exposure to such things at too young an age would open doors to sin. I truly don't know. I didn't know for a long time.

The first inkling dropped when a friend of mine gave me some "guys devotionals" for my fourteenth birthday. Targeted for those in the heat of puberty, all three books were exclusively about sexual purity. (Christians love to talk to high school boys about what to do with their penises. In church, purity is highly stressed to middle school boys. As a result, we tend to forget to mention that they were made in the image of God. So often we'd rather them know about abstinence and forget to tell them they are beautiful, godly, and worth so much. I wonder why that is.) I remember an entry was about a young man who felt aroused one afternoon in the locker room around his male friends. The section assured me, the reader, that with such strong hormones, we shouldn't be scared if those homosexual (this isn't gay! Just homosexual) feelings occur, and we'll outgrow them.

"Okay," I remember thinking, "this is normal. This will pass."

It's funny; I don't remember anything else those three books said. No wisdom or truth comes to mind when my eyes brush past those devotionals. I can only recall this lie the author gave me. Did he want me to suppress my feelings? He may as well have said . . . well, anything! Anything else would have been more helpful. Just ignore what we feel? How absurd! Though I understood, and maybe even agreed for a time that ignorance is the easier route. Don't talk about being gay. It's tricky. It hurts. It's too awkward. You have a lot of people to win over in this life, bud.

Life will be easier if they don't know this about you, if they don't know you.

SEVENTEEN YEARS OLD

Opening up has been hard, but the value life offers in deep, vulnerable friendship is too wonderful to ignore. When I'm alone, even the church tells me to run: run to help, to friends.

As a gay man, having another man mentor you within a Christian sphere where homosexuality isn't condoned is a strange thing. Sharing life, praying together, laughing, telling one another intimate things: these can be arousing for a gay guy. One piece of advice is to run! Run some more. Run from temptation; do everything you can to flee from sin!

So I run from these arousing moments to isolation, where the dark parts of my life are no longer being brought to light, and I have no one to confess to or ask for help. It's terribly lonely, and a little horny there. Run! Run to the light! The church shouts at me ("Run" is a common thing to shout at the high school boys when they admit to feeling horny). All this running is making my heart beat out of my chest. Good Lord, I'm out of shape.

If you're unfamiliar with the subculture that is evangelicalism, I apologize. What I'm getting at here is to be a gay man immersed in the evangelical church is to exist in a grey area where most people only know of black and white.

No, it is to *be* the grey area, and to desperately need to be understood. I'd give anything for a mentor nearby who is willing to exist in that grey area with me.

I used to have one. His name was Ryan.

Ryan took me under his wing when I was in seventh grade. He was nineteen and about two heads taller than I at the time. Someone who saw that I wasn't as happy as I let on got me to start meeting up with him. I never quite opened up to Ryan the year we met up, but he was always patient and kind even when I did nothing but seemingly waste his time.

He'd ask me about life, my family, my struggle with anxiety and depression. I'd respond, "things are going good."

Things were always "good" when I was thirteen. We would sit in a tense silence facing each other for the next thirty minutes, and would make arrangements to meet again the next week. This went on for a year until he moved.

Sometime when I was seventeen, I apologized to Ryan, and wished I had taken more advantage of our time together. He took that apology and ran with it. He pushed me to make up for it by talking now, and I will never thank him enough.

Over text and phone calls, he began to explain to me what I was experiencing sexually. We still spoke about it broadly, mind you, but that was illuminating enough for one who still literally did not know what sex was.

That's a preposterous thought, isn't it? I didn't look at porn, and still haven't. I wondered if that was why I was still so uneducated. Had everyone around me really had in-depth conversations with parents and loved ones about sex, or had a majority found out about most sexually-charged information through pornography? These questions made me feel a little more righteous. My ignorance was strength.

Ryan always shined lights on my sexual ignorance with loving and appropriate expansions. I was beginning to learn and understand my humanness in a beautiful way because he decided to have some awkward conversations with me. Genitals are a good thing! Sexuality is a good thing (but don't tell the local youth pastor . . . not yet).

I can see now the whole scenario was entirely God's kindness that he would put someone in my life—even long-distance—whom I could trust so intensely. I would ask him anything I didn't understand, and he answered with kindness and patience. Over the phone, my seventeen-year-old self was beginning to learn that trusting someone who is praying for and advising me was deeply freeing. That feeling didn't last long though. After a few of these sessions, I was beginning to grasp how and why I felt the way I did. Each day, denial and repression were harder to achieve. I tried to intellectualize it. "This doesn't mean I'm *completely* gay," I thought, "I'm going to grow out of this." These thoughts were hourly battles in my mind until one day, during one of our conversations, Ryan asked three words that forced me to confront everything: "Are you gay?"

"What? No," I replied quickly. I didn't want to face it. I couldn't face it. I wasn't ready.

Silence.

He knew. He was waiting.

I wanted to be loved. I still do. I'm sure you do, too. I want to be admired, enjoyed, and sought after. I want to walk with my head up in prestige, not wondering if someone is remembering the rumors of my past. Until this point, I was willing to live a lie for the sake of those around me, and for my sake. Talk about porn with six seventeen-year-old guys at a bible study, and you may hear some earnest perspectives and maybe an irreverent joke or two. Talk about homosexuality with six seventeen-year-old guys at a bible study, and . . . actually . . . I don't know what you'd get. Probably most people don't know. Maybe I should try that sometime.

My mind raced. I couldn't say anything else. It took every ounce of courage to stay on the phone with him, but the quiet indicated his patient presence. He loved me. He was listening to me.

"Yeah, I think so, Ryan."

"I'm gay too," Ryan said.

A long, awkward conversation followed, in which he talked and I listened. I had said all I could that day; admitted all I could handle to admit. Over the phone, I couldn't see him, but I know that he was entirely earnest when he ended the conversation with, "I love you, Collin."

I appreciate that now more than ever. He never hinted that being gay was easy. He never promised God would "heal me," only that I was loved.

I said, "Okay," and hung up. He knew what I meant.

Looking around to make sure no one was listening in, I put the phone back in my pocket. Was this relief? Not quite. I was shaking. Was this fear? Maybe a little bit. I don't know how to describe what I felt at that moment other than "myself." Maybe for the first time. What a terrifying thing to be.

I had said out loud the thing I would have rather died than say. I looked around; I was still here. It didn't kill me. Maybe my racing heart was just pumping far too much adrenaline, but my reflection in the mirror shone truer, a little brighter.

But none of this description can do that moment justice, the moment I finally faced myself. Let's try this . . .

Succumbing to death, I wasn't anticipating taking another breath. I couldn't face the storm, and below the surface of the water seemed so much more peaceful.

"This is a better way to die," I had thought, "than getting struck by lightning or a wave breaking my neck."

It was as if my head finally surfaced from the ocean as a storm pushed the waves higher and higher. I took in another breath. I braced for impact, closing my eyes because every horrific end I had anticipated was too much to bear.

And all of a sudden, silence. Stillness.

I was in the eye of the storm. The roughness was still in sight, but here it was calmer and quieter. Just for a moment, I could hear myself breathing, catching my breath. Even salty air tastes infinitely sweet when you had thought you were done tasting air altogether. The air was just as salty, just as sweet that moment with Ryan when I lived that honest moment in my body.

But still, as I looked at the storm which would cover me again eventually, I couldn't imagine this was going to have a happy ending.

EIGHTH GRADE

The peak of any insecurity finds itself most corruptive in middle school. Even the kindest child turns into a monster for at least some moment during those horribly pubescent years. Friends would smirk at seductive rumors about other friends, if just for a second. Anything to alleviate one's own self-loathing and ever-changing body was welcome, no matter how bitter it tasted afterwards.

This agony was only intensified for Ana and her classmates, who attended a school which combined both middle school and high school students. Not only did she have to deal with her flat chest becoming slightly less flat in the peripherals of similarly-suffering eyes, but she also had to walk into school every day next to women—beautifully presented, attractive women, who drove themselves to school. Women who were applying to college, working jobs, and even tossing around the rare post-graduate con-sideration of marriage.

And that was nothing compared to the men. Eighteen and nineteen-year-old men who were popular, tall, and had zero braces on their teeth. There were a few who were so large, Ana only came up to roughly their belly button. To consider them her peers was laughable. To consider herself a subordinate to all of these almost-adults was to live in fearful reverence and walk with her head down. Her eighth grade classmates all felt similarly.

The camaraderie ended there, however. Ana was more and more a loner. She never invited people to come over to her house, and that tended to be reciprocated. It was fine, though. It always seemed that what Ana lacked in friendship was made up for in popularity. Everyone was friendly with Ana, and she was widely admired. For a middle schooler, Ana found herself involved in no conflicts, which is a huge feat for any 14-year-old girl to achieve. No one would think to believe Ana was lonely, except one girl.

"Hey, Ana" Melody Price said with a comfortable smile, "you coming over this weekend?"

"I think so."

"No!" Melody said, getting a little more assertive, but still smiling, "You ARE coming!"

Ana laughed. She was the queen of flaking out of plans, and Melody's insistence burst through her usual defenses. Ana found herself especially flaking when it involved church. She was begin-ning to suspect that this trend made her even more sought after. May the best Christian win.

The past couple of years had left her less optimistic, and more skeptical of people, especially in the religious world. She now saw into what seemed beautiful, and sensed the trap. They could turn on you at any moment. Make a single mistake, and be devoured.

"We'll pick you up around 6:30," Melody said before Ana could get in another excuse.

The youth room was lit up with stage lights and sound equip-ment worth more money than Ana would need for her entire col-lege career. The other kids were loud—no, booming. Booming with laughter, worship, shouts during games . . . it seemed like no matter what they did, they did it booming.

Melody was kind enough to sit close to the back so Ana could spectate a little more easily without being in the middle of it all. It was the first time Ana had been to church in at least a couple of years.

"Had it really been that long?" Ana thought to herself. Her racing heart, which had slowly sunk into her stomach, would make her think it was just last weekend that she had sat in the pews. It felt far too familiar. She kept a watchful, wary eye on everyone as best she could.

Melody never left her side. She declined helping greet guests that night because "I'm already greeting a guest, and she's right here!" That meant the world to Ana. It seemed as if Melody could sense the uneasiness. Her anxiety was tangible tonight.

And before Ana knew it, the youth service was over.

"Wasn't too bad, was it?" Melody offered.

"No, not too bad."

"There's someone I want you to meet. She's basically the coolest person here."

Melody pulled Ana across the crowd of a few hundred middle school and high school students until they found an older woman, maybe in her early 30s.

"Elliot! This is Ana."

From the moment they met, Ana could tell Elliot was the most confident person here. She was shorter, had war paint on from the game they played that night, and wore a camo headband. Under all of it, her olive skin was still radiant, and her piercing green eyes didn't seem as young as the rest of her. They carried wisdom and discernment, and seemed to read a person as easily as a book.

"What! Is THIS the Ana we've heard so much about? And you've brought her here on the day I decide to come as a grape?" Elliot gestured to her hair that poured down a little past her shoulders.

The hair was dyed silver, but was beginning to turn purple, as Elliot explained, from too much purple shampoo, but somehow it made her even more beautiful in Ana's eyes.

"It's nice to meet you," Ana laughed a little awkwardly, " . . . haven't been to church in awhile."

"Woah no way!" Elliot said, without a hint of judgment in her voice. It was an exclamation full of empathy and admiration. She knew immediately this was difficult for Ana. "What did you think?"

For the next hour Elliot offered as many questions as she did input. When Ana shared something extra profound, Elliot would utter a little "Oh yes. Wow." She thanked Ana when Ana gave a little piece of earnest information about her background. She laughed louder than anyone Ana had ever heard whenever she or Melody would crack a joke.

Ana learned that Elliot was married to a man whom she kept referring to as "my big idiot" and that they had a son together five years ago. She referred to him as "my little dummy."

When it was far past time to go, and they were some of the few people still left, Ana realized she'd shared everything with not only Elliot, but Melody too. Both were safe presences, utterly delighting in Ana. All of a sudden, she didn't want the night to end.

"Oh, Ana!" Elliot yelled as she hugged her not too tightly, but Ana wouldn't say she could have gotten out of the grip very easily, "You and Melody HAVE to have a girls' night or something soon."

"Yes! That would be amazing," Melody said.

Ana all of a sudden heard a plan she didn't want to flake out of.

"Okay," Ana said a little nervously, as if getting too excited might make this reality disappear. Had she found a friend and a mentor in one night? Could she finally talk to someone about all of the hurt and loneliness that life's circumstances had caused her?

She couldn't wait for next Wednesday.

CHAPTER 3

As I PROCEED WITH my story, I am a bit overwhelmed. I want concision without sounding cliche; I want to encourage you without indulging in unrealistic expectations.

The truth is, as I am choosing to remain celibate, I am grieving something that will never be and has never been. In some ways, it's a different sort of grief than the loss of a loved one; in other ways, very similar. Depending on how psychologically flexible I am on any given day, I am malleable to both hope and delusion.

I begin to think, "This won't always be the case. My circumstances can change in an instant."

I'm not great, but I do believe my God is. He can change me in the blink of an eye. But, can he actually? Can even omnipotence change the "unchangeable" while keeping me intact? Can even something all-knowing answer impossible nonsense? What if he has created my life to suffer?

These questions and thoughts crumble in on me as a tunnel caves in on a miner digging deeper underground.

"I will never know a lover," I think to myself as I roll over in my half empty queen-sized bed. Even if I am surrounded by friends all day, I will go home to an empty house. My friends will get married and have their own priorities. I will be left in the dark.

"Is the Gospel enough for you?" If you ask me this, you're definitely a Christian, and almost certainly know who John Piper is. I may roll my eyes, because it is enough, and it most certainly isn't.

Go ask the starving homeless man the same thing as you purchase your venti coffee. Ask the social outcast if Jesus is enough as you make plans with your friends for the evening.

I think sometimes you ask this because you know my fears are inevitable. You don't fight my fears of loneliness because you have no intention of suffering that fate with me. You sound both condescending and dutiful. I get it, but I don't know how to answer your question.

Sometimes it seems that Christ is my provider the same way that a prison provides food for its inmates. He gives me resources I didn't earn in order to do work that does not seem significant or meaningful at all. At the end of the day I still go back to my cell. And when I cry, I cry alone.

TWENTY-FOUR YEARS OLD

I don't really want to live anymore. My eyes glaze over even as the thought crosses my mind. It's not a passionate thought. It doesn't have fire behind it. It just is. Its monochromatic greys dampen every sign of life as it sits in the corner of each room I walk into; it's always following, never quite demanding my attention, but always present.

I don't really want to live anymore. I'm bored. I gather the energy to talk to God. I reflect on my day. I got paid more than most to work a job I love, and then did exactly what I wanted to do the rest of the evening. Privation has never been a worry of mine.

I don't really want to live anymore. I saw my family tonight. They're wonderful, hilarious, and heart-forward. I have a great time. I lie in bed and somewhere in my sleepy thoughts, just before losing consciousness, I think, "If I never woke up, that would be amazing." I keep waking up, half annoyed and half wondering if I might be immortal.

I don't want to live anymore. I think I've peaked. Not in every way, but in the way of how much I enjoy life. Friends keep getting married, having babies, pursuing romance. It will always be their priority. What are my priorities?

I don't really want to live anymore. I call the thought a demonic lie. I am made in the image of God, and the weight that concept carries is much more than the cliche it bears. I have unimaginable light and life inside of me.

But it's not a lie, and I don't think it's really even demonic. No. It is more a holy tension, much like a wrestling with God. I want to face this thought every time I have it, not repress it. I want to challenge it and challenge God and be given a new name and life.

I want to shake loose of this, much like a snake sheds his skin and leaves it behind to turn to dust. I want a lot of things. But tonight, as I write, I mostly just don't want to live anymore.

EIGHTEEN YEARS OLD

You might call it confirmation bias, but the less I tell about myself, the more people celebrate me. I look back on this past year, my senior year, and see the game high school taught me to play. As long as I don't cuss in front of the wrong people, I can keep singing at church and worship services at school (because charismatic Christian high schools . . .). I am voted "Mr. Christian Leader" on superlative day.

If I am funny and cool enough, people will look up to me. I mentor five middle school/high school guys from affluent families because they seem to want something I have.

If I don't express my sexuality, or ANY sexuality, then I can keep being the leader everyone makes me out to be. I am voted Homecoming King.

If I am kind, and believe what is expected of me to believe, then I can succeed. I am voted "Senior of the Year" by the staff.

My identity is as transactional as any other thing that's mine. I am straight so that I am loved, so that I can be invited to the thing next Friday, so that I can sing on stage during worship. This isn't the duality of man; this is picking a different man altogether and insisting that it is me. No one seems to question it.

I remember that Saturday night when I was crowned Homecoming King. I wish I could say I was surprised or humbled, but I wasn't. It felt like the kind of thing I had inadvertently campaigned for my whole life. Never making a conversation about myself, always checking up on people, trying to make the outcasts feel seen and the popular kids feel valued for more than what they could bring to the table: it was all a brilliant disguise which used kindness and care to hide my own needs and vulnerability. (A natural 2w3 for those of you who like the enneagram.)

The more I made someone see himself, the less he'd wonder about me.

The people applauding and truly recognizing me felt good for a moment, but I still had to feign the smile.

"Which of you would love me if you knew who I am?" I asked. "Is it worth finding out?"

SIXTEEN YEARS OLD

I stand on the stage with reverent posture; the musicians begin as I inch my face closer to the microphone. My heart is racing as usual, although not because I'm nervous to sing. He's in the crowd, not disengaged but looking up rather blankly. He's taller than most.

I begin to sing.

"All to Jesus I surrender . . ."

I wonder how he feels about me.

"All to him I freely give . . ."

I wish I could rest my head on him—just once.

"I will ever love and trust him . . ."

His hands.

"In his presence daily live . . ."

His chest.

"I surrender all. I surrender all . . ."

His smile.

"All to thee my blessed savior. I surrender all."[1]

I'm hard.

I smile because I was told it's important to express joy when you're leading people in worship.

---

1. Van DeVenter and Winfield S. Weeden, "I Surrender All," public domain.

Every note I sing is a juxtaposition between the internal and external melodies somehow both pounding away inside of me. Perplexing enough, my spirituality and sexuality both thrive as a spotlight warms my face. They hate one another. I shove that reality aside as I lead everyone in a prayer.

EIGHTEEN YEARS OLD

I heard a spoken word recently that dealt with the shame the woman at the well must have felt. For those of you who aren't familiar with the story: Jesus talks to a promiscuous woman who was not unfamiliar with the shame of her past. The woman would go to the well in the heat of the day (as opposed to early in the cool morning) simply to avoid the eyes of other women. When asked about her past, all she offered Jesus was that she was not currently married (which was true, she had been married a few times, and the guy she was with now was not her husband, which would have made her a HUGE outcast in Samaria, where she was).

Of course, as Jesus often does, he makes her feel seen, and loved, and does not judge at all, but offers her a life that doesn't carry the weight of secret shame on her shoulders.

Jesus acknowledges her guilt, and offers her a lot more than her shameless neighbors have. The chorus of the poem references how well Jesus seems to know her, "To be known is to be loved, and to be loved is to be known. I want to be known." One can not exist without the other. To say you love someone without even knowing their name would be absurd.

"I want to be known," the poet says as she reflects on this story. Of course, you might infer that Jesus offers us the same love that he gave the woman at the well, and I'd agree. In fact, that is one of the reasons I myself am able to write about my life the way I do.

But the satisfaction in being known and loved by our God is not going to stop me from challenging us all to do more. In fact, it empowers me.

I love what the woman did in response to meeting whom she believed to be the Messiah, the Savior. She ran back to town. I imagine she ran even to those who wanted nothing to do with her. She wanted them to meet this source of life, this thing that took the weight of her identity off her shoulders.

I want to be known.

TWENTY-THREE YEARS OLD

The Advocate: A Poem

Being in the closet, even as a celibate gay Christian, has rendered me unable to defend myself whenever other Christians unknowingly hurl hurtful comments my way. The risk is palpable should I ever choose to provide insight into homosexuality as I experience it, therefore it has become invaluable to let someone advocate for me. Not only do I get to feel safe and defended, but the culture shifts when another person says, "Hey, that would be hurtful for a gay person to hear."

For me, this advocate is Trey Celaya, the author of the foreword to this book. The following is a poem I wrote while reflecting on how essential he has been to my survival—my survival even from careless comments shot at me like arrows from close friends.

The Advocate . . .

His gentle demeanor makes anyone feel warm and safe, empathy personified. His smile is neither assuming nor expectant; he is just in this moment with me. Whatever this moment is, it is. It simply is.

You may make assumptions about him. "He isn't very bright." As if a slowness to speak and an honest list of questions indicates ignorance.

"He's kind of lazy," as if decisiveness is always a good thing.

Some of you might see him and assume something very different, but it doesn't really matter to me.

He's The Advocate. He lives outside of me, and when my mind is too much to bear, and my identities close in on me, I look through the cracks between my fingers at him. A calm in the storm, flesh around what I thought I'd only find in concepts or in God. He's a peace beyond understanding.

He doesn't pull the hands off of my eyes, or ask me to calm the storm (which of course I cannot do) but waits with a steady heartbeat and warm arms until I'm ready to face what I could not face before he arrived.

He is a defender, with sword and shield in hand, he is a wall that allows nothing unsafe to come through.

Even my allies, who have mistaken me for an enemy, are unable to shoot their bows past my advocate's defenses.

Eventually they see his colors and know that both he and I are on the same side. They see there were no enemies to begin with.

He is a recruiter. Knowing there will come a day he will fall, or will sleep too deeply into the night for my rescue, he makes more advocates.

He trains them, correcting their stance and strategies. He teaches them what their previous training had ignored. The recruits are better for it, and I'm safer until I'm surrounded.

And when my body has reclaimed enough strength, the advocate hands me a shield of my own. New allies help me get to my feet. The shield already feels lighter than when I first held it. He points to someone in the distance.

"How long have they been there," I ask. "Awhile," The Advocate says simply.

I've never noticed them before, but I run to them. I neither notice nor care how much energy I exert, but I seem to catch my breath quickly.

"Do you need an advocate" I ask the stranger, shield in hand.

TWENTY-TWO YEARS OLD

Poem: The Cell (written after a particularly long panic attack)

I stand in a cell, grasping for anything before the panic takes over. The confusion begins all over again, and I can't even remember how to breathe. Is anyone out there? Whatever I'm sitting on is cold and vague. I'm alone. Will no one help?

Wiping away tears and catching my breath, I try to speak.

It seems like we have very different opinions of what freedom is, God. Because if your Spirit is inside of me, and "where the Spirit is, there is freedom," then something is not adding up.

The anxiety attack is making coherent thoughts almost unattainable. I gag from crying too hard.

My arms and torso begin to shiver, or are my muscles trembling from so much panic?

How dare you put me here, God. If everything is in your control, you could have prevented this. You could have made this doable, survivable.

But haven't I survived? Haven't I done it up to this point? I am shivering, but not frozen. I am hungry, but not starved.

I pause for a second. The voice sounded like mine, but the words were different. They came out much easier, much calmer.

I can't do this alone much longer. I think it's literally impossible.

He will never leave me.

How do I trust that when I'm falling apart?

Listen.

How do I do that, God? You are not here. I need a solution, not some idea that changes as I change.

Collin, listen.

If you're actually all-powerful, this is a pretty pathetic display of your power: one of your "dearly loved" sons dying alone in agony. Sometimes logic tells me you're either evil or powerless.

Silence!

I feel a gentle breeze. This is no cell. Am I outside?

There's a dancing light, a fire. It looks miles away, but undeniably inviting. Are those people?

There is a warmth interrupting the darkness. I can start to make out the earth which I'm standing on.

Dawn is coming.

10TH GRADE

"May I go to the restroom?"

"Sure, Ana," Mrs. Richardson answered.

Ana stood up, noticing that Mrs. Richardson's eyes followed her all the way from her desk to the door. She kept doing that.

"If you want to say something, say it" Ana thought, "creepy bitch."

Ana pulled the sleeves of her fleece down past her wrists. Ever since her study hall teacher caught a glimpse of the marks, it was like she was a different person.

"How are you doing today Ana? What have you been reading lately? Oh my gosh, I LOVE that series."

There was no escape. It was a hug that wasn't like Elliot's at all. It was suffocating, and absolutely uninvited.

"I'm sure she's just worried about you, and wouldn't you be?" Elliot had asked.

"Sure, but just, like, either say something or don't. This weird passive aggressive game is so uncomfortable."

Elliot gave her a concerned, loving look as she listened, and Ana thought maybe no one was on her side. Elliot had been her mentor ever since meeting Ana in 7th grade. She met with Ana and her friend Melody at least weekly, often more than once a week. There were sleepovers, vacations, coffee dates . . .

Between Elliot and Melody, Ana felt that she had all the friends she needed.

Ana set herself on the toilet and locked the stall. She pulled up the sleeve to her shirt and gazed at the marks. There were five parallel, fading marks on her wrist that kept her attention for a few minutes before she proceeded to slice a fresh cut a little lower than the five were. It was easier to conceal if they were lower.

Ana closed her eyes and began to breathe a little slower. She sighed a few sighs of relief, keeping her wrist level with her heart before finally relaxing it. The rage and anger seemed bearable. Serenity enveloped Ana for a few seconds in that bathroom stall.

And just like that, it was gone. The world turned grey again; nothing excited Ana. She felt sad still, angry even. What had just invigorated her seemed to leave her void of every ounce of energy and passion. Cutting was always a sharp reminder for her that escape does not mean deliverance from any confusion or pain. No, what she always hoped was a symbiotic relationship only left her with self-loathing and even more mess. She looked around her stall. What a pathetic waste of time! She was still sad. She hated herself.

She needed Elliot. Ana needed her mentor's hands on her. The only time Ana had ever felt safe and secure was with her. Elliot had first tried spending the night in the same room as Ana when Elliot's family was out of town. What they did, Ana could not say, but Elliot warned her that they would both be in massive trouble if anyone found out.

Ana didn't want anyone to find out, to begin with, though. Elliot was her safe place, her mother figure that she'd never really had with her own mom. Maybe Ana could see if Elliot wanted to dinner later that night.

CHAPTER 4

TWENTY YEARS OLD

As I ENTERED MY college years, I was a young adult who was still partially in denial. I knew I was gay, but my mentor at the time had told me that if I had enough faith, God would eventually "heal me of it all." It shouldn't even stop me from trying to date a girl and get married! I'm not sure I ever believed that for myself after high school. Maybe for a time I did, but so often I see that God's faithfulness seems to be in sustaining someone rather than fixing them. It's a bit like cancer in that there is peace, humility, and beautiful redemption during the battle, but not always a cure. Strange.

Depending on the day, depression still flared up like an allergy, but it was never crippling. I was busy enough to never dwell on it for too long.

Dating had never occurred to me as a possibility. I was realistic and wanted to put my Christian convictions before anything else, but like every other young adult, the need for intimacy was always in the back of my mind. It is funny how those seem to contradict so often: my understanding of what God wants for me, and what I feel I need.

One spring semester, I decided to take a night class. This night class in particular left me frustrated on a greater scale than most three-hour night classes, mostly because it took place on the night when movie tickets at the theater were only five dollars instead of eleven. As a college student working a minimum wage job, missing out on a discount like that was a huge blow. More than once I considered skipping class if my friends were going to a movie that I wanted to see, but almost always chickened out . . . almost.

At first, I was excited to learn about my psychology class. The way humans interact with themselves and each other has always seemed like a crucial piece to understanding the mechanics of love. To me, it makes God a lot more personal and beautiful when we look at each individual psyche, seeing various strengths, passions, shortcomings, and tendencies in one another. To my disappointment, general psychology turned out to be more about theorists and personality disorders.

There was one interesting lecture, however, regarding a theorist named Erik Erikson. He theorized that, through every stage of life, we have particular obstacles to overcome. In his explanation, he asserts that without overcoming the obstacle in each phase, we can't adequately find health in the next. In adolescence, it is self-identity versus shame. Early in life, children will fight inferiority and, hopefully, come out knowing that they can learn and achieve something. At this point in my life, as a secure young adult, Erikson believes I will chase intimacy and overcome isolation.

It was an interesting thought experiment, connecting isolation and intimacy to my relationships. Pain from intimacy, to some extent, is unavoidable in any deep relationship that lasts long enough, but Erikson believes that mentally healthy adults will accept that people are worth our enduring that pain. Intimacy is always a risk.

I'm regularly skeptical of theorists in psychology. In my narrow understanding and exposure, the theories tend to conflict, convolute the obvious, or just explicitly reflect a depraved and jaded mindset. But regardless, Erikson had an interesting thought—fear of intimacy might lead to my isolation.

Between classes as the weather warms up, I lie out to tan. My bedroom window connects to a flat part of my house's roof, and is just convenient enough to entice me maybe three or four times each year. Every time, I am encouraged to find out that I'm not narcissistic enough to withstand the Southeast Texas humidity just to achieve a tan. Maybe I am just too high-maintenance to be in the sun that long? My inhaler and I have never given off the illusion that I was much meant for outdoors. Either way, weeks pass, I forget the heat on the roof and try again to tan.

I bring out my speaker, and a towel long enough to protect my entire body from being scorched by the sun-baked shingles.

In this particular tanning session, I remembered a recent encounter on my way to class. Spring had sprung into the air, and every organism on this green earth had been particularly . . . springy. There on my path, a couple of birds landed right in front of me for a noon-day tryst. It's like they were showing me what I'd been missing!

Call me a prude, but I thought it was inconsiderate and downright crude of them. Should I have shooed them away or just kept watching in horror? Is it courteous to look the other way? I've never been good with those types of social situations, especially when I'm caught by surprise. But you know what they say: birds do it, bees do it too. In fact, if I had to guess, I would say a lot of bees were doing it near my roof while I was lying in the sun, listening to music, and trying to enjoy myself despite the miserable heat. One bee in particular was especially active.

He was a large fellow, hovering about five feet away from me. Aside from his size, he was a pretty typical looking specimen, but I've never seen such personality in a bee. When other flying insects, fellow bees, or even birds came close, he would dart after them and chase them until they were a good distance away from the roof. (I'm not sure if the birds were scared, or if they had just decided there was nothing on the roof that made pissing off the bee worth it.) He wasn't a very smart bee. I named him Albert.

Albert kept this up for about forty-five minutes while I occasionally glanced over to make sure he was still a good distance away from me. I'm not sure why he let me into his roof kingdom undisturbed, or why everything else seemed to be a threat. I liked to imagine that everything Albert was doing was all an effort to make my hot, sweaty roof a little more enjoyable. The more he let me inspect him, I realized that he didn't have a stinger. Could he even defend himself when he encountered a threat?! His defenselessness made his personal-security-guard demeanor even more endearing.

My little bee would occasionally circle around the perimeter, making sure every corner was entirely secured. I would hear him faintly buzz as he chased the crows away, and I began to wonder if he had a hive somewhere. Where was his partner? Do bees even have partners? Maybe he was protecting my roof so his family could move in. Oh Albert, if only you spoke more than Bzzz.

As I continued to wonder about my bee friend, I forgot about the heat. The fact that my hair was drenched in sweat escaped my mind. In my discomfort, I could at least feel relaxed, and a little amused. Here a strange bee had embraced me as one of his own. Who knows? Maybe if this friendship could blossom, I'd have body guard bees AND honey thrown into the deal. I've heard local honey is good for allergies. I smirked under the sun, and my speculations for the future continued. I thought about Erikson again. I imagined defending my isolation to him: "I have a close friend right *here*," I'd say as I gesture toward Albert.

Somehow I doubted my contrived friendship with Albert would make a very convincing case to prove intimacy in my life and may even be very concerning for a psychologist to hear.

I opened my eyes. The mood had shifted. The buzzing sounds increased in both pitch and volume. All of a sudden, Albert bolted across the roof. Perhaps he saw a bird to protect me from. Maybe his family had finally made it to his new pad and, in his excitement, he had doubled the speed of his patrol. All I know is that he flew right into my lower back, inadvertently head butting me. In his deep sense of duty, Albert couldn't maneuver accurately.

Despite his lack of stinger, Albert was still a bee, and that bee drew a little too close to me, so I killed him.

I looked at the shambles my panic and insecurity had caused. My smirk disappeared; the possibilities for Albert and me ceased unfolding before my eyes. It wasn't making me smile anymore. The joke wasn't funny. I decided it was time to go inside and wash off, maybe watch TV or something.

As Erik Erikson's question of intimacy and isolation seared into my mind, my loneliness became difficult to ignore. It became clear that I was isolated, and nothing would change unless I changed it. I was twenty at this time, and decided to call my closest friend, Seth Carter. He was the first guy in my life who held a friendship with me. All my close friends had been girls.

Looking back, I certainly made do without male friends, but is that acceptable? Why did my survival make it tolerable that no other male my age at church wanted to be around me in any significant way? It's what happens when unbiblical forms of masculinity become the expectation—in-groups and out-groups are created, and individuals are haphazardly thrown in the margins. This is another way the church had failed me. Up to that point, any significant dynamic I had with another male was them taking me under their wing to mentor or counsel me. I appreciated that mentorship, but it was an incredible privilege and answered prayer to have a friendship on equal grounds with another guy. I never experienced that until two decades into my life.

Seth is a Christian, and aside from that, we have nothing in common. Since I've known him, he has always been incredibly athletic, good looking, kind to a fault, soft-spoken, and extremely introverted although you wouldn't think so at first glance. Naturally, I am none of those things. At times, he has even been almost twice my weight. I often joke that we really shouldn't be friends. At a glance, we simply don't seem compatible to be as close as we are, but it seemed God had other plans. We met when he was a senior in high school. I was a freshman in college at the time, and we instantly had a close bond. Our love for irony, theology, Game of Thrones, and coffee brought us together in powerful ways.

When Seth started attending the same university I did, he asked if we could meet up regularly. With our mentor Trent, we began to meet at least weekly, pray for each other intentionally, and hang out regularly.

I felt like the luckiest guy in the world to have a friend like Seth. I'll never forget studying in my living room together one night as we both took on a full load of classes. We didn't need each other's company, but we both preferred it.

After a period of silent reading, he looked up at me with intent and perhaps a touch of apprehension.

"I have been reading about King David and Jonathan," Seth said.

I looked up, letting him know I was listening.

"It said they were so close, and describes their souls being knit together." There was a pause in Seth's voice as he continued. "That's how I feel about us, Collin. When you're in pain, I feel the pain. When you're happy, I am too."

I sat in his words for a moment before I replied. "Yeah. I feel that way too, Seth."

Satisfied with my response, he went back to his book. A man of few words indeed, but undoubtedly powerful words.

After a few years of this, I had confided in him everything except my battle with homosexuality. For awhile I thought, "I'll give it time. I need to see if I can trust him with my smaller things first." As the years went on, I became more afraid. How would Seth be okay with my waiting this long to share such an important part of me? I decided that there was nothing aside from my pride keeping me from disclosing my confusion with sexuality to Seth. I texted him that he should swing by my house briefly. I needed to talk to him about something.

"Okay, I'm on my way." Seth knew me well enough to recognize that whatever was going on was important to me. I'm sure I seemed off, even over text.

My heart was pounding. I was about to lose my best friend. It seemed inevitable to me. Seth would be there in five minutes, let me stumble over my words while I confessed the things I was most ashamed of, and then politely back away. It was becoming hard to breathe. During trips together, we had shared a bed on multiple occasions; would he be angry that I did that? Would he immediately assume that our friendship was built on lies or a secret crush I had on him? I wondered how much I was going to have to clarify or explain. My mind raced. I was beginning to have a literal panic attack.

He arrived, and I walked outside and sat in his car. I jumped right into what I had to say. It couldn't wait any longer.

"You know how there are times when I'm depressed, and nothing seems to trigger it? I just get really sad?" I managed to look him in the eyes.

"Yeah," he replied slowly. It was an urge for me to continue. I was visibly terrified, and he knew it.

"Well a lot of that is because I struggle with homosexuality." My voice was trembling, and it was all I could get out before I put my head down and began to weep.

One thing to understand about Seth is that he processes things differently than most. He is extremely intelligent and nurturing, and is a deep thinker, but would prefer not to express his heart in verbal soliloquies. If he is expected to fish out the right words quickly, he panics. I knew that going into this conversation. He put a huge hand on my back as I cried. Seth didn't speak much that night, but with no hesitation, he was there with me. It spoke volumes more than his knowing the right things to say ever would.

"I hope this doesn't change anything between us," I said through tears. He assured me that this didn't change a thing.

Intensity of the moment aside, we both had class early the next morning, and couldn't linger. We sat in silence for awhile before he hugged me and I went back inside. I had finally opened up to someone who was near me, and I didn't regret it. I was excited for the intimacy that comes with being known and loved by a brother in Christ. The feeling was more than relief; it was freedom. I am not certain, but I think that Erik Erikson would have been proud of me. I texted Seth that night, and told him how grateful I was for the kindness and love he had shown me.

It would be a few months before he would reply.

FOURTEEN YEARS OLD

Towards the beginning of my teen years, I idolized one of the older guys at my school. His name was Remy Simmons. Remy was a sophomore, drove a BMW, sang and played guitar like a pro, came from a good family . . . you get the picture. Everyone knew his name, especially the girls. For some reason, he had decided to single me out to take under his wing. Whether through text, hanging out, or phone calls, I constantly was in communication with him.

With only a few restaurants and a mall to drive to, our conversations were the driving force behind our friendship. I confided in him much, especially when it came to how often I felt sad. It was good to have a friend I admired praying with me and checking up on me, but mostly pointing me to the Lord. I never had a talk with Remy about anything personal that didn't end with prayer. Remy always reminded me who the Wonderful Counselor actually was. Conversations also led to absurd jokes, light gossip, and, you know, friendship things. That's what I'm getting at. We were friends.

"You have a real calling on your life, bud." Remy told me as we browsed Dillard's. "Your singing and worship leading is so anointed. Keep honing that gift."

It was a compliment full of hyper-spiritual phrases that didn't mean much to me, but I accepted it nonetheless. He continued.

"Let me play guitar for you and we can work out some vocal exercises to keep you in shape. You need to try to stretch your range even further . . . oh."

He froze. There in front of him were two men, one with his hand on the other's lower back. With fingernail polish and atypical haircuts, they kissed and continued to browse the shoe department. I watched the two lovers smile at each other as they walked.

"I'm sorry you had to see that," Remy said, as he shook his head once the two lovers were out of earshot. He was distraught and heavy-hearted. "I just wish we could still handle things like in the Old Testament, and stone the gays to death." As he was about a head taller than me, he looked down to make eye contact, and patted me on the back, as if to comfort me from the trauma of it all.

"Yeah," I replied. I didn't say much else the rest of the day. I wonder sometimes if he'll ever know who had actually traumatized me that afternoon. I wonder if he'll understand that my fear of intimacy comes from comments of the same vein, which feign holiness while condemning something so misunderstood.

I wonder if I fear intimacy because you fear me.

FIRST YEAR OF COLLEGE

It was one of those moments which felt so repulsive, so foul, that there is no language for it. Ana's heart skipped a beat as she listened to her best friend Melody speak.

"It was all God's plan," Melody said again, "to make you stronger and wiser. I could never have gone through what you did and still be the incredible role model that you are. I love you, Ana."

Melody smiled as she finished. To ask Ana now what Melody said would be switching on what seemed like a speechless rant—flabbergasted, yet with so much to say.

It was all God's plan for Elliot to have raped Ana? What an ignorant and horrible thing to say. As if Goodness himself would orchestrate heinous trauma just as a means to make someone stronger, to teach a lesson? As if the Creator of Time is simply bound by his creation, trying to make the most out of every passing minute? No, he is instead of time. He has already overcome evil. It is won.

The weight of such an assertion as "the God who saved Ana was also the God who raped her" is not just simple impotence, but disease and rot. How it could ever be helpful, Ana wouldn't know.

Ana had finally seen a counselor about the years of sexual abuse she had endured from her mother-figure Elliot. Telling Melody for the first time that their mentor Elliot had raped Ana was to relive every shame Ana had ever felt. It was Elliot their mentor—the woman who prayed with them; the woman who counseled them sometimes multiple times a day; the woman who took them out to eat on their birthdays and when school was out.

To have Melody not believe her was to relive every moment of shame alone. Ana didn't press it, and walked away crying. Elliot was Melody's mentor too after all. Melody insisted Ana was making "mountains out of molehills" and something from the past was being misinterpreted.

"She has raped me . . . for years" Ana ended the conversation stoically as she had proceeded to turn around and walk away. Tears erupted as soon as her face was out of Melody's sight.

After news had spread, Melody wept an apology, and Ana had been trying hard to forgive her. It was easy for Ana to understand intellectually: the news and shock were too much to make their way into Melody's reality, so she rejected them. There were still some subtle lies making their way into Melody's paradigm, but Ana had her own sorting out to do for now.

Convincing people, she decided, was not her job. Everyone seemed to side with Elliot automatically.

"But she is like my second mom," friends would reply, processing the news.

It felt human and natural to initially respond this way, but it still stung. Ana was the one who suffered. Ana was the one who didn't get any choice in what she believed about the accusations. She lived it. There was only one true story for her.

Her parents were driving down to campus to see Ana tomorrow . . . another conversation that Ana wished would never have to happen. All of the navigating, the conversations, the comforting . . . they were slowly seeping their way into each day.

It was exhausting, but she found herself thanking God more often for her life. The weeks recently were not restful or joyful or even good, yet something within her was serene, stabilized.

Things aren't going well, Ana thought to God, but they sure as hell are a lot better than they were.

Ana walked toward her dorm as she reflected. Her strides were a little more sure lately; her eyes no longer looked at her feet as she stepped; she stood about an inch taller.

CHAPTER 5

TWENTY YEARS OLD

THE WEEKS AFTER MY confession to Seth progressed at a painfully slow pace. At first, his absence wasn't anything to note. He becomes a recluse pretty regularly, indulging his introversion without any warning, and I knew that he may need some time to process such an emotionally charged conversation.

"Would you want to hang out today? Maybe watch a sermon at my place?" It wasn't an uncommon request. We did that together regularly. We loved to watch Matt Chandler preach at The Village Church in particular. "How's it going, Seth?" I asked a few days later. Still no reply.

"You know, I told you something about myself that I'm deeply ashamed of. I confessed something that often makes me consider killing myself, and you won't even acknowledge me. What's going on?" I texted with tears in my eyes after two weeks of silence.

"I just need some time, Collin."

So a month passed by. I began to feel less than human. Seth's reaction verified what I had already suspected: that no Christian could ever both know and love me. I was angry, but more than that, I was desperately hurt. I wanted so badly to forgive and move on, but Beaumont, Texas, isn't huge, and inevitably seeing Seth in passing made shame and sadness well up inside of me in ways I couldn't have imagined were even possible.

This man I considered my best friend, and even a brother, couldn't offer a single conversation with me about my sexuality. Is this how all Christians would react? Perhaps everyone who knew I was gay up to this point had decided to keep a safe distance from me, but I just hadn't noticed until it was my best friend.

During these months of silence, I would take long walks down Beaumont's Hike and Bike trail. It is roughly two-and-a-half miles of unlit path through classic Southeast Texas marshlands. It is not in the best part of town, and anyone who went there late at night was up to no good. I would walk for miles into the early hours of the morning almost every night to pray. At least, that's the reason I told myself. I think I half-hoped something bad would happen to me.

"God, why is this happening?" I would ask, usually with more expletives. I prayed as I walked in silence. "Please, just go ahead and take me," I wept. More mostly incoherent half phrases would fall out of my mouth as I put one foot in front of the other.

I laid on a bench to look at the stars. Screw the stars. Screw Seth. I felt numb at best. I didn't care about creation. I didn't care about my life. The only thing I was painfully aware of was how tired my legs were from walking so much. There were creatures scurrying around me, but I didn't investigate. Nothing peaked my interest. No mystery was worth solving. Before standing up and treading on, I sat up to write.

SILHOUETTES: A POEM

I was walking down a trail I could hardly see. The only light guiding my way was that of the moon. It's just a reflection of the sun, but even its allusion to something I couldn't see was enough to illuminate my way.

The few feet in front of me were all I needed. In the four miles I trailed, I couldn't see the end until I had reached it. Each twist and turn was a mystery only solved when I was ready. It was a long few hours of tears and prayer and listening, but with each step, I saw the next one I needed to take.

There were times I sat down and rested. I lay down and closed my eyes, wondering how much longer I had. My knees ached, and my eyelids grew heavy, but I turned my head and saw the next few feet of trail before me. Completely visible. Completely doable.

I was totally alone, save the thicket around me. The silhouettes of trees and brush to the left and right served as both scenery and boundaries. They reminded me why I stayed on the path, why I wasn't cutting through in an effort to make it easier.

Completely void of color or depth, they could've been two dimensional for all I knew. Their shape was clear, but that was it. The darkness filled in the outlines of branches and leaves, but only the first layer of them.

I couldn't see what was behind the shrubbery, what perhaps was inside the forest enveloping me. But the thought alone implied there was something out there to be found. The signs of life were irrefutable.

But even inspiration seemed absurd to try to feel for more than a minute. Under a cloud of anger and hurt, there was no life to be found in me. I wasn't going to last much longer.

How dare he? This friend I spent my time with every day for years, how could he turn his back after making it clear that I needed him? I wouldn't wish this feeling on my worst enemy. I was furious, bitter, perplexed, but most of all heartbroken. Not only could he not comfort me anymore, but he refused to talk about why he couldn't at all be present. With no opportunity for reconciliation or even closure, a restless, angry grief more than stung. It ate at me daily.

I was angry at Seth. I was angry at myself for being so foolish to believe my life could ever work out. I was angry at God as well. How could my "loving Father" let this happen? If everything is ordained by him, how could he ever allow my sexuality and happiness to be so skewed to the point where I didn't have a friend in the world? Every night, I wrestled with God on these questions as I, sometimes hysterically, trekked down the path.

At the peak of feeling so unjustly wronged, I began to realize something. Seth was a Christian, best friend, and intimate brother. But he didn't owe me anything. I was not entitled to his time, his friendship, or his help. My panic was coming from an expectation I placed on him, not on something that I was guaranteed. I could rationalize and argue that the Bible commands us to weep with those who weep, and mourn with those who mourn, and that we are supposed to live for each other. But the grace and forgiveness that I offer can't be contingent on how well those commandments are carried out by other people. I definitely still loved God, and can honestly say, even in my anger, I was beginning to love Seth again.

It was a humbling time that broke me, but in the midst of fury and hurt, I sensed God was still teaching me much and loving me fiercely.

After a few months of either silence or cold, polite exchanges, Seth asked to talk. He saw me in passing, and, perhaps moved by my stoicism towards him, texted me that he was ready to have a conversation. Maybe he was getting lonely too.

That night, we met on the same trail that I had cried and prayed on so many times the past few months. All of the times that I had asked for reconciliation, cried for hope, and prayed for relief were soaked up on that route. Both my mourning and praise echoed in the trees, and it was only fitting that we met there to address what beget so much of my struggling. Besides, I'm sure the critters lurking and watching me throughout the whole process wanted to see how this story would end.

Seth was waiting at a set of picnic tables. I came and sat on the other end, not offering any type of greeting or words of acknowledgment. I was the quiet one for once.

"I fucked up," he said with a crack in his voice. I remained silent.

"You've been such a good friend, and the second you needed me, I was gone." He looked me in the eyes, but I couldn't match him. I began to cry.

"Do you realize how much you've hurt me?" I asked, every pent up emotion beginning to seep out. I explained to him what the past few months had felt like for me. I told him stories of the pain, the silhouettes of the trees, the lonely questions, the tearful rage . . . I asked him why it had to happen.

"I don't know," he said after taking a long moment to think. "It was hard and scary for me, and I have been incredibly selfish. When you needed me most, I only thought about myself. Will you ever be able to forgive me?"

The wind was blowing, and I could hear cars flying down a country road in the distance. I was still staring at my feet. His explanation wasn't good enough. I wanted to know more. I looked up and, for the first time since I've known him, saw tears in his eyes. Maybe he said all he was able to say for tonight.

"I'll try, Seth." This began my healing.

Over the years, Christ has taught and is teaching me an astronomical amount through Seth about forgiveness, grace, patience, hope, perseverance, and so many other things. He has needed to forgive me as much as I have needed to forgive him. I'm not sure we'd have grown as close without the aches we both went through. God made beautiful things out of our contention and mistakes. As the story goes, it turns out there's no person to this day I'd rather confide in than Seth.

There is something so necessary about having friends who know my battles intimately, and I'm more than thankful to experience it with someone after so many years of isolation.

I've occasionally wondered what Erik Erikson would have said throughout my whole experience. Would he tell me that Seth isn't worth the pain, heartache, and time I spent? Would he encourage me to move on and search for people who love me the way I am, or would he be happy that we worked to eventually see things through? I don't know. Actually, I couldn't even tell you off the top of my head if Erikson is still alive. I do know what God says about love, however. I know that his love endured.

Singer-Songwriter Sara Groves writes,

"Loving a person just the way they are, it's no small thing. It takes some time to see things through. Sometimes things change. Sometimes we're waiting. We need grace either way. Hold on to me, and I'll hold on to you. Let's find out the beauty of seeing things through."[2]

I believe the greatest love I have for a friend has been birthed from Something sustaining me as I endured more pain than I've

2. Sara Groves and Gordon Kennedy, "Loving A Person." Sara Groves Music, 2005.

46

ever experienced. A friend who has been willing to, as Groves sings, find the beauty in seeing things through with a love that believes, bears, hopes, and endures all things.

It's almost as if, through all of the pain, suffering, and perseverance, the story of Christ was made even more poignant for me. Maybe even mirrored in some ways. I can imagine that Christ dying on the Cross felt pretty hopeless. I wonder how his mom wrestled the next three days, after being promised her son would save us all. Hopefully it was with a similarly steadfast anguish.

CHAPTER 6

I sit across from a man older than me with my arms crossed and voice timid. He gives me a comfortable smile as we wrap up our talk.

He has just finished telling me that the sins I struggle with don't change how he looks at me. Whether it's heterosexual or homosexual sin, it's still all sin.

I think he's trying to be understanding, letting me know that I'm in a safe, level-headed place. I want to stop him there, though. Why does he assume that because I'm gay I'm in sin? Even if I believed practicing homosexuality were a sin, I just explained to him that I am celibate and have never even glanced at pornography.

The message he's conveying is that I am in sin because my desire, not practice, deviates from the norm. The sinister precedent has already, probably accidentally, been laid: that because I'm gay, I have something to apologize for. My desire for men is equally as bad as a straight man living a promiscuous life. I reject that. Should I explain it to him?

"God still uses single people," he encourages me.

He's an elder at a local church. It's a prestigious honor that only straight married men can receive at this particular location.

I smile back and nod. He is right. I'm not sure he actually knows why he's right though. This week, I have had the time to teach my lower income neighbor how to drive so he can get to his new job on his own. I have the freedom to pay my acquaintance's bills this month after she's already had a few panic attacks about making ends meet. I have been a shoulder to cry on for 3 different college students after I get off from work.

This week, this man sitting across from me has had the time to nobly tend to his wife and newborn, and have this talk with me. He needs to end our talk early.

I concede that he probably couldn't handle more details anyway. You start getting a sense for who lives in a world of strict binaries and who doesn't. The latter group are the ones who can meet me in the grey area that is a celibate, faith-filled sexuality.

They're the ones who can listen when I describe my need for intimacy with other men, and they're the ones who will help me experience it.

They're the ones who will lay their head on me and let me know they love me even when I accidentally get aroused.

They're the ones who find duplexes to invest in so that their gay friend can live close by and share family dinner with them every night.

They're the ones who will challenge their own paradigms just for the sake of empathizing with me more profoundly.

This man sitting across from me, who heard me confess my most vulnerable secrets, gives me a fist bump then makes his way to his car. Other than to qualify himself as a more adept and well-rounded Christian, I wonder if he'll ever think about our conversation again.

TWENTY-TWO YEARS OLD

I am training to be a speech-language pathologist. Presently, I have three of five semesters under my belt, which means I've given a little over one hundred hours of hands-on therapy.

It's a humbling experience, to fumble around as a first-year graduate student. "GIVE ME A KISS," a kid on the autism spectrum screams at you as you desperately try to redirect him to the first page of a storybook you've had opened in your hands the past 10 minutes. Your supervisor looks over, most likely knowing that the battle is lost today, but still expecting you to fight through the next

15 minutes of therapy. You leave that day, knowing you'll return the next day to try again and again until the semester is over.

I have learned this year that all of the knowledge of theory in the world can't help me manage the behavior of a child better. It's just not in me. I simply was born without the instinct.

Despite the insipid therapy sessions I provided, my clients have moved me more than they'll know. Even if I am not cut out for the behavioral therapy they need, their pain has changed me.

During one semester, I had prepared a cookie activity for a client of mine. I'll call him Bradley. These types of sessions work out great because kids will never fail to be excited about cookies and will do anything for rewards as satisfying as sweets. Not only could I reinforce turn-taking and eye contact skills, but this would develop use of descriptive language without Bradley even knowing. "Is the cookie sweet or sour?" I could prompt him. Bradley was an elementary school child with autism who was completely nonverbal. He was brilliant, and communicated using a writing pad. He was often fidgety, but always engaged me during our sessions.

That day felt different though.

I took his hand and brought him into the therapy room. He was frowning. "What's the matter, bud?" I asked.

Bradley frowned and looked up at me, but pulled me to our table to get started.

"Look what I brought for us today. Cookies!" I held them up. He didn't respond. He began to cry.

"Bradley, can you tell me what's wrong?" I gestured to his writing pad until he took the pen.

"Lights" was the only thing he wrote.

"Is there a problem with the lights?" His severe OCD sometimes got in the way of therapy, but the solution was usually as simple as putting the lid on the toilet or cracking the door open slightly.

Bradley started to scream and sob inconsolably. His school teacher ran into the room, and tried the same strategies I tried before simply hugging him and walking him outside until he could calm down.

I stood in the corner helpless.

What was I supposed to do? I am quite literally training to help with these exact problems, and I couldn't even stop Bradley from becoming hysterical.

I sat in silence a few minutes before the door cracked open again. A puffy-eyed Bradley staring at the floor walked into the room.

"Hey, friend!" I said. My eyes were a little puffy at that point too.

He came, and pulled his chair next to mine. I asked him if he wanted a cookie, but he began to cry again and shook his head. He put his head on my shoulder and hugged me. I hugged him back. We cried together for the rest of the session.

In any sense, I could not and will never understand what went wrong that day. I do not understand whether he hated the cookies, the flickering lights, the burnt-out bulb, the list could go on and on. My mind reeled that entire week, trying to determine how I could have helped. All little Bradley was able to communicate was how he was feeling, not what he was feeling, but maybe that was enough for that session.

Yet the thought bore down on me: "You were supposed to be the expert, Collin."

I was supposed to be the one to understand how to help. Of anyone there, Bradley's success was my responsibility, and I failed. I hadn't prepared enough. I was too incompetent. I didn't guide the therapy session correctly.

But perhaps no . . . Let's say I was not the expert. Let's say Bradley was. In all my self-awareness, maybe I had forgotten who else was in the room with me. There were two people sitting at that table, both playing a role, and maybe Bradley handled his emotions exactly as he intended to. That I felt helpless to lead did not matter to Bradley. He understood exactly what he was feeling. He led me.

I might even venture to say there was a certain strength at play in his vulnerability.

When everything else became too overwhelming; when his environment or his thoughts were too much of a barrier to communicate a solution, Bradley put down his head and wept. And when he was escorted out of the room, he insisted that he shed his tears with me and not alone. By the end of the session, he left smiling.

I wasn't smiling, though. I loved him. Why did he have to deal with the things he dealt with? Why was something as simple as a cookie-tasting game impossible and traumatic? Why couldn't he use the toilet without sending a scout to be sure the toilet seat was down?

All I could do was hold him and cry. But that's all he asked of me. In his moment of weakness that day, he demanded to be with someone, even someone who clearly didn't understand him.

He couldn't hear my pleas for clarity over his sobs, but he knew that I was present; he knew that I was attentive . . . that I cared. Whatever his needs were, they were met through a trembling grad student who was as scared as he was unsure of how to help.

And how often do I myself identify with his autistic tears? My questions and pondering, as usual, are met with silence. I thrash and scream as much as Bradley. I remind God that I ask similar questions about myself. Why are often the simplest things so overwhelming to me? Why can friends and mentors find me in a fetal position sometimes multiple times a month, and have to hold me in their arms for hours while I mourn and panic over my sexuality and loneliness?

I get no answer, and I can produce no answer. The anxiety and sadness and loneliness overwhelm me. I can't tell my friends, much less myself why it happens in the form of such waves. In the same way I am a helpless onlooker for Bradley as he fights tooth and nail to have a normal life, my loved ones feel helpless to console me. They don't have the treatment, diagnosis, or even the experience to understand what is happening to me, so they endure my snot and tears and screams.

And I agree with them. It's not the cure. I will still deal with this tomorrow. Yet somehow my needs tonight were met in the arms of a friend. I can walk away inexplicably alleviated by one's presence. No truth need be spoken, just the silence and arms of someone who loves me. I can't explain it, but all I can say at the end of the night is "thank you" with new strength.

The next day in therapy, Bradley beamed when I came into sight. He held my arm and smiled straight ahead as we walked down the hall. Bradley wrote "I love you" on his writing pad. He wouldn't let therapy start until I wrote it back to him. He made significant progress that day.

"Where two or more are gathered . . . "

TWENTY-FOUR YEARS OLD

It is now 2019. I'll try not to get too meta, but ending this book has been looming over me. I want to leave you all with a sense of hope, conclusion, or even a stance, but I can't quite do that.

Not yet. I need to address my Christian readers, because there's still work to do.

There's still work to do. The Southern Baptist Convention just recently put out a resolution that states I'm no longer allowed to call myself gay, even if I remain celibate and Christian. I optimistically can say it is probably to affirm that my identity is in Christ, and not in sexual preferences, but I don't feel optimistic. They don't want their paradigms to be challenged by someone as atypical as me. They want my language to be as suppressed as the existence of my sexuality. I politely refuse.

There's still work to do. When gay Christians are still being hushed by their churches, it means we're not to be heard or seen. We will be pushed further from faith or deeper into secrecy. The sexual minority will remain in the margins, starving at the hands of those who most loudly preach the love of God.

There's still work to do when single gays who are trying to live a life in submission to God don't even have someone to put down as their emergency contact at the doctor's office, even though they are deeply involved in a church community.

There's still work to do when Christian families, who in their sin would refuse to let a gay person enter their house, are not called to repentance and change by their pastor or friends.

There's still work to do when a congregation is satisfied with their straight minister who, in his pride, attempts to write off or understand the sexual minority with a three-point, fifteen-slide sermon that he spent a few hours Googling the week before.

There's still work to do when most of my shame, rooted in things out of my control, is spurred on by the Church.

I have my doubts the conversation will ever be safe, that I'll ever be able to navigate this safely inside church walls. I have doubts that I'm even making the right choice in celibacy. Are the songs I sing on Sunday even true?

Forget about the church for a second. Is my God who I think he is?

There have been some worship songs and scripture that I physically haven't been able to utter because, if they're true, then I'm angry that I often seem the exception.

If they're not true, then things feel pretty hopeless. One example is "surely goodness will follow me all my days" (Psalm 23:6).

This strange, perhaps unholy tension ushers me closer to him the same way a conflicting current and breeze can usher a boat along its voyage if it is angled the right way.

Inexplicably, in my irreverent prayers to challenge God to make sense of it all, to stop seeming so passive, to "screw this bullshit," to accomplish what so many stress he could easily do; in my bitter tone, not unlike Jonah who wanted to go ahead and die instead of endure what seemed so unfair, in that headspace and the challenges I shout to the sky, I encounter something that always proceeds from my tense-faced prayers: a peace I can't pin down.

So I'm going to keep shouting for now. I'm going to lean into what I'm feeling, believing in my unbelief that I am not alone—and I don't think I am alone.

I'm going to yell into the darkness, f-words intact, until something bold enough scrapes against something true enough to spark a fire.

ELLIOT

Elliot flushed her throw up down the toilet, wiped her mouth, and, for the first time that day faced herself in the mirror. She was struck

COLLIN BRICE

at how the reflection didn't look beautiful anymore. Her now dark blonde hair seemed pale and unkempt. Her dull eyes looked neither innocent nor wise. And her posture over the sink as she tried to collect herself appeared witch-like.

She heard her husband and now ten-year-old son in the next room watching TV. It had been a day since she received the call. Ana would be pressing charges for the years of "child molestation" that had occurred. She couldn't look in the mirror anymore.

She had acted as Ana's mentor for almost ten years now. No one knew her more intimately than Elliot.

Her life was behind her. She was going to die. That sounded much better than facing this, actually. Significantly better. She was now the outcast, the criminal that no one ever dreams of becoming. And what about her other mentee and dear friend, Melody? Would she ever get to see her again? Would Melody ever forgive Elliot once she found out that she was a . . . *rapist*? She shoved the word back before it made its way into her inner monologue. It wasn't one she wanted to hear or even think about yet.

Looking her husband in the eyes and telling him everything seemed unbearable. What would he do? What else would he ask?

Every new speculation sent Elliot through another wave of wails. She had to step into her car so no one could hear her. And what about her son? What would they tell him? How will everyone at their church treat him?

She turned the car on and thought about running it off the road, of letting the garage fill with fumes until she slowly passed away. Wouldn't that be better for everyone anyway?

She rested her head on her steering wheel, paralyzed both with the fear of doing nothing and a fear of doing something.

"A fire," she heard herself say.

She should just light a fire and burn in it. Elliot thought about Joan of Arc, burning at the stake for the sake of something bigger than herself. Not quite what Elliot was going through.

She imagined the Godly men in the Bible, who were thrown into a furnace, but not burned at all.

She thought about Hell, and how many times it had been preached as a horrible, everlasting torment full of fire.

"I'm going there," she said out loud. It was a submissive tone, not full of grief but of acceptance.

She thought about all the good things done, even for Ana. All of the times she had talked young girls out of horrible mistakes, counseled mothers and fathers who didn't know what to do with their kids anymore, prayed with families who had lost everything.

"A fire," she felt again.

She didn't need another hint. The fire was coming; it always was. She hadn't guessed the trail of smoke was for her. It was a wildfire, killing communities, devastating neighborhoods. Elliot was always the one guiding others through it, through their sin and mistakes. As she had reminded so many others, she was still made in the image of God. She was human, a creature designed to be god-like themselves—to rule, to be glorious.

Let the fire come, she thought, to refine me. Bring the smoke, ashes, tears, and blood until I look nothing like myself, and then heal me. Sew my flesh together again, and let these veins flow through a heart that isn't heavy or calloused. And when it's all over, bring me peace.

"Okay," Elliot whispered. The thought was incomplete and foreboding, but it was enough to face this day, this hour, this next minute.

She switched her car off, got out, and turned to face the fire.

FINAL THOUGHTS

Wow. You did it! We're here at the end.

You have made your way through The Acre, and although you've probably realized there's much more to discover here, my tour of it is over. You have helped me confront and even survive the misshapen monster who sought to devour my story and my secrets. You let me take your hand and show you both what I hate and love about this place, and I could not be more grateful. Each snapshot of my time spent sowing and reaping and watering this land has reminded me of where I've been and where I am heading.

It is a wonderful, poignant, and illuminating tension as I see how each moment of loneliness, each tense conversation, each realization, each cry for something different or easier, and each story has led me here where I am now. As I reread entries, I often don't recognize the man writing them. I find myself different—wiser, happier, sometimes sadder. As I turn and look at the trail behind me, there are far too many twists and turns to retrace my steps adequately. I am grateful for the time spent recording this journey, because it's easy to forget that I wasn't always as supported as I am now. I'm quick to forget how hard it once was to face myself in the mirror at all. Lord, help me remember. Help me remember that there are those who are now where I once was.

And this is where I stop talking about myself.

I can't offer finality, but is there even such a thing? I want to give you something much more realistic and useful: a benediction.

It is a sacrament in the church which signals to the listener that the holy moment and words are over, and it is time to reflect. It is time to stand up, and walk away. It's time to spend the day with loved ones, hopefully changed by what you've heard. It is time to consider, to quiet yourself and listen for the gust of air that reminds you you're not alone.

It is time to receive something . . .

So to the bisexual young woman who has hidden half of her sexuality from her loved ones so that she can maintain her worship leader position at church . . .

To the gay man who never even had the opportunity to consider spirituality because the doors were slammed in his face too quickly . . .

To the ashamed mother who is wondering if there's anything she could have done differently for her struggling transgender child . . .

To the abused college student who has never been able to view the church or intimacy as anything but a threat to his life . . .

To the skeptical Christian who has begun to deconstruct her faith in a search for something real and accessible and life-giving . . .

To the straight husband who has realized marrying a gay woman is much more complex and difficult than he had wanted to admit . . .

To the queer "exvangelical" who tried to make Christian faith work so long before finally deciding that the panic attacks and mental breakdowns were too much to endure . . .

To every reader who has found themselves annoyed, confused, defensive, moved, bored, or sad throughout this book . . .

May the God of goodness and clarity move your questions, uncertainty, and ambiguity to a place where life and love animate you. May He empower you to embrace the grey parts of your world in ways that are both challenging and refining.

May goodness and empathy nurture your thoughts until all of the difficult blessings and the universal pain which connects human experience serve to alleviate your existence instead of antagonize it.

And while those lifeless and dead things are restored in ways that not even my imagination can describe, may you turn to your neighbor and help them do the same.

Lightning Source UK Ltd.
Milton Keynes UK
UKHW022034060422
401213UK00011B/132